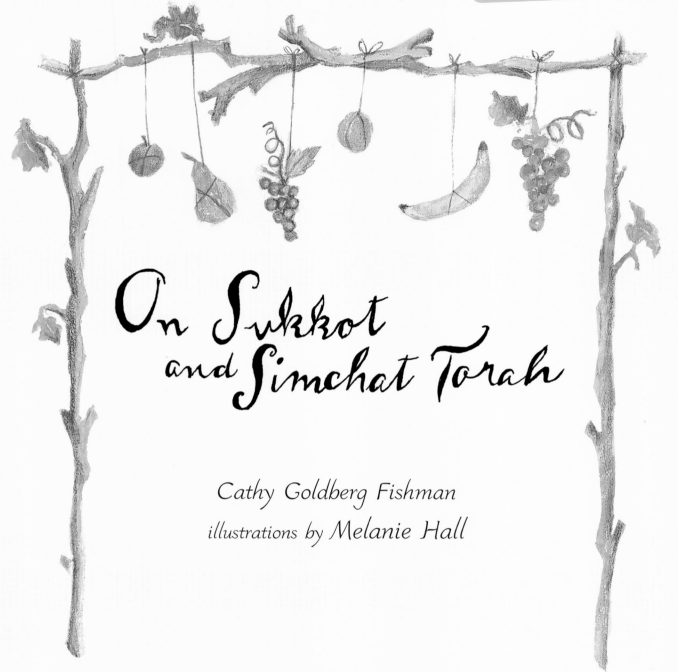

On Sukkot and Simchat Torah

Cathy Goldberg Fishman

illustrations by Melanie Hall

KAR-BEN
PUBLISHING

KAR-BEN PUBLISHING, INC.
A division of Lerner Publishing Group
241 First Avenue North
Minneapolis, MN 55401 U.S.A.
800-4KARBEN

Website address: www.karben.com

Library of Congress Cataloging-in-Publication Data

Fishman, Cathy Goldberg.
    On Sukkot and Simchat Torah / by Cathy Goldberg Fishman ; illustrated by
Melanie W. Hall.
        p.   cm.
    ISBN-13: 978–1–58013–165–0 (lib. bdg. : alk. paper)
    ISBN-10: 1–58013–165–4 (lib. bdg. : alk. paper)
    ISBN-13: 978–1–58013–166–7 (pbk. : alk. paper)
    ISBN-10: 1–58013–166–2 (pbk. : alk. paper)
    1. Sukkot—Juvenile literature. 2. Simchat Torah—Juvenile literature.
[1. Sukkot. 2. Simchat Torah. 3. Holidays. 4. Fasts and feasts—Judaism.]
I. Hall, Melanie W., ill. II. Title.
BM695.S8F57 2005
296.4'33—dc21   2001022789

Manufactured in the United States of America
1 2 3 4 5 6 – JR – 11 10 09 08 07 06

To Steven, with thanks for the sukkah of love he
constantly spreads over our marriage. ——C.G.F.

For my uncle and aunt, George and Roz Sandel,
with love. ——M.H.

"Who wants to help?" my father asks, as he drags long pieces of wood into the yard.

"We do!" we all shout.

Yom Kippur is over and it is time to get ready for Sukkot, the Festival of Booths.

My brother and I start to nail the wood together.

"This sukkah will help us remember that we lived in small shelters when we escaped from Egypt," my mother reminds us.

"It is a mitzvah to sit and eat in the sukkah," my grandfather adds.

My mother and sisters hang canvas from the frame to make walls. My father and grandfather place cornstalks and pine branches on top. We hang fruit from the leafy roof and paint pictures on the walls. We put up lights and bring in tables and chairs.

It feels good to be busy after the thoughtful stillness of Rosh Hashanah and Yom Kippur.

We gather in the sukkah on the eve of the holiday. My grandfather explains the custom of ushpizin, inviting our Biblical ancestors to join us each night of the holiday. "Tonight, we are inviting Abraham and Sarah," he tells us.

"Come in, holy guests,
Please join us in our sukkah.
Please come in patriarchs,
Enter matriarchs.
Take your place with us
And join us at our meal."

Rebecca

Jacob

Leah

I imagine them walking into the sukkah
and sitting beside me as we eat.

Abraham

Sarah

Isaac

I can feel the cool night breeze come through the canvas walls and smell the piney scent of the sukkah roof. The full moon and stars shine through the branches and the swaying fruit shimmers in the light. They remind me that Israelite farmers used to build booths during harvest time. I imagine them eating and singing as they gave thanks to God for a good harvest. The sukkah surrounds me and I feel peaceful and safe.

*I*n the morning we put on sweaters and gather in the sukkah for breakfast. Before we eat, my father says the blessing over the lulav and etrog and hands them to each of us to shake.

I cradle the yellow, bumpy etrog in my hands and breathe in its lemony smell.

My brother counts the branches of the lulav.

"One, two, three, four, five, six."

"That's right," my grandfather smiles. "One palm branch, two willow branches, and three myrtle branches."

I turn my face to the morning sun and carefully hold the etrog in my left hand and the lulav in my right hand. I say the special blessing and shake them in all directions: east, south, west, and north. I even shake them up toward the sky and down toward the ground.

"Why do we shake the lulav and the etrog all over?" my brother asks when it is his turn.

"I know," I answer. "On Sukkot we remember that God is everywhere."

Every day we eat our meals in the sukkah. And in the afternoon, I like to do my homework there.

Sometimes we play games and read. And when the weather is warm enough, we even sleep there.

In synagogue on Sukkot mornings, we parade around with the lulav and etrog. The branches rattle together and bits of the leaves fly around me. I can smell the goodness of fruit and sweet leaves in the air.

My rabbi says the lulav and etrog are like all the parts of a person.

"The etrog is like the heart," he says, "and the willow leaves are like lips."

I look carefully at my lulav and listen to the rabbi as he continues.

"The myrtle leaves are like eyes and the palm branch is like our backbone. On Sukkot we try to remember to worship God with all of our heart, all of our soul, and all of our strength."

At the end of Sukkot is a holiday of its own called Shemini Atzeret, which means the eighth day of coming together. In synagogue, we say special prayers for rain so that the next year's crops will be plentiful.

"I'm going to miss Sukkot," my brother says.

"I will miss it, too," my grandfather agrees, "but tonight we have another holiday. Tonight we celebrate Simchat Torah. All year long, we have been reading from the Torah. Tonight, we finish and start at the very beginning again."

In the evening, I watch as the rabbi opens the ark. I see all the Torah scrolls inside, with their white covers and silver decorations. One by one, the rabbi takes them out. He hands one Torah to my father, another to my grandfather, and the rest to other members of the congregation. They carry them around the synagogue seven times. My brother and I march behind them, waving flags and singing. Many people in the congregation join hands and dance, joyfully weaving in and out of the line.

At last, all of the Torah scrolls are carried back to the bima. It is time for us to listen as the Torah is read. My mother gets the honor of chanting part of the Torah. On Simchat Torah, the children get to help, too. Four tall men hold a large tallit over us as we sing the blessings.

Everyone in the congregation listens quietly as my mother begins. I stand near her and watch as she moves the shiny silver yad, like a pointing finger, over the Hebrew letters in the Torah.

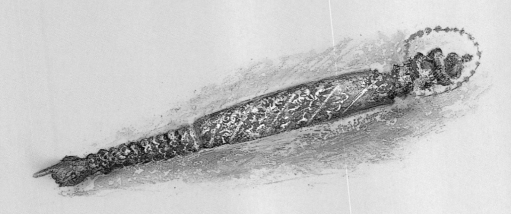

My grandmother says that, if you put together the very last letter and the very first letter of the Torah, it makes the Hebrew word "lev" meaning, "heart". My mother reads the words of Torah in a beautiful, melodic chant. I think the rhythm of the chant sounds almost like a heartbeat – a heartbeat made from the words of Torah that have given life to the Jewish people for thousands of years.

After synagogue, we go home and I stand in the empty sukkah. The harvest holiday is over. I imagine that the ushpizin and the Israelite farmers wave goodbye as they go back to their homes. It is time to take the sukkah down, but I know that next year we will celebrate again.

We will build a sukkah and remember our ancestors. We will wave the lulav and etrog and give thanks for our blessings, and we will gather in the synagogue, dancing joyfully with the Torah, as we celebrate Sukkot and Simchat Torah.

Glossary

Bima – the podium in the synagogue from which prayers are led and the Torah is read.

Etrog – citrus fruit symbolic of the harvest

Lulav – palm branch bound with sprigs of myrtle and willow symbolic of the harvest

Mitzvah – commandment

Rosh Hashanah – Jewish New Year

Simchat Torah – fall holiday when the yearly reading of the Torah is ended and begun again

Shemini Atzeret – a holiday following Sukkot when the prayer for rain is recited

Sukkot – holiday celebrating the harvest and recalling the booths the Israelites lived in during their sojourn in the desert

Sukkah – harvest booth

Tallit – prayer shawl

Torah – first five books of the Bible, a compendium of Jewish law and history

Ushpizin – traditional Biblical guests who are symbolically invited to the sukkah to celebrate

Yad – the pointer used to read the Torah

Yom Kippur – Day of Atonement, observed ten days after Rosh Hashanah

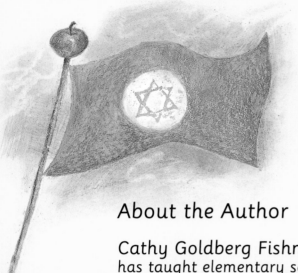

About the Author

Cathy Goldberg Fishman, a graduate of Lesley College, has taught elementary school, run a daycare center and owned a children's bookstore. Her previous children's books about Jewish holidays include On Passover, On Rosh Hashanah and Yom Kippur, On Hanukkah and On Purim. She lives in Augusta, Georgia with her husband and two children.

About the Illustrator

Melanie Hall attended the Rhode Island School of Design and received her B.F.A. from Pratt Institute. She has illustrated over 25 children's books, and has received numerous awards including the Parents' Choice Award for outstanding children's book. She teaches children's book illustration, and lives in Olivebridge, NY.